Teens and Drinking

Other titles in the *Teen Choices* series include:

Teens and Drinking

Gail B. Stewart

TEEN *Choices*

ReferencePoint Press®

San Diego, CA

For more information, contact:
ReferencePoint Press, Inc.
PO Box 27779
San Diego, CA 92198
www. ReferencePointPress.com

LIBRARY OF CONGRESS CATALOGING-IN-PUBLICATION DATA

Stewart, Gail B. (Gail Barbara), 1949-
  Teens and drinking / by Gail B. Stewart.
     pages cm. -- (Teen choices)
  Includes bibliographical references and index.
  ISBN-13: 978-1-60152-910-7 (hardback)
  ISBN-10: 1-60152-910-4 (hardback)
  1. Teenagers--Alcohol use--United States--Juvenile literature. I. Title.
HV5135.S755 2016
362.2920835'0973--dc23
                                                                    2015018998

Contents

A Choice for Teens

When Carrie was in eleventh grade, she was invited to a party that was to be held after a Friday night school basketball game. She was excited to be asked because she was new to the school. Her family had recently moved to a suburb of Detroit, Michigan, from a small town near Raleigh, North Carolina. Eager to make a good impression, she brought a batch of homemade brownies and a gallon of ice cream.

Soon after her mother dropped her off at the party, however, Carrie realized she had made a mistake. As she recalls, Marin, the girl hosting the party, took one look at what she had brought and began to laugh. Carrie explains:

> She thought it was hilarious that I was bringing brownies and ice cream, while everyone else had brought some kind of liquor—beer, vodka, hard cider, and stuff like that. She told me I could probably find someone who would share their drinks with me. I felt stupid. I didn't know that everybody drank here. I mean, I knew kids drank back home, but they were older, like seniors. I will always remember Marin saying, "*This* is how they party in North Carolina?"[1]

Carrie, now twenty-two years old, says that the humiliation she experienced that night still bothers her. She says:

> At the time, I was mortified, like I had committed a giant social error. I was mad at myself and even madder at

my mom who was the one who suggested baking the brownies. And instead of being "that nice new girl who brought cool stuff to the party," it was like I was in third grade. So what I did to feel like I belonged with these new kids, and to feel like I was more grown up, was to get drunk like the rest of them.[2]

But now, five years after that party, another aspect of the experience bothers Carrie even more—the fact that she chose to drink at the party. She had not engaged in drinking before that night, and she is still annoyed that she decided to drink simply because she was embarrassed. "It was a stupid decision," she says. "Not the only one of those I've made in my life, but it was a choice made pretty much strictly to fit in, even though I knew it was the wrong choice for me."[3]

> "She thought it was hilarious that I was bringing brownies and ice cream, while everyone else had brought some kind of liquor."[1]
>
> —Carrie, a seventeen-year-old newcomer to her high school.

A Difficult Choice

Carrie knew at the time that her drinking that night was motivated by wanting to be liked and accepted by her peers—a common reason why teens make the choice to drink. Millions of teens—and people even younger—make that same choice, even though it is illegal in the United States for anyone under age twenty-one to drink. In fact, according to the Centers for Disease Control and Prevention (CDC), alcohol is the most widely used drug by youth in the United States.

But although it is a popular choice with many teens, underage drinking can have serious repercussions, besides the illegality of buying or consuming alcohol. According to the National Institute on Alcohol Abuse and Alcoholism (NIAAA), alcohol is responsible for a yearly average of 190,000 emergency room visits for underage drinkers. And each year, approximately five thousand young people die as a result of

Although underage teen drinking is illegal, it is a common occurrence. One strong motivating factor for drinking is the desire to be liked and accepted by peers.

underage drinking—from alcohol-caused motor vehicle crashes to drowning, falls, and burns. Too, these underage drinkers are more likely to carry out or to become the victim of a physical or sexual assault.

With so many possible dangers associated with drinking, it may seem surprising that so many young people are making the choice to drink alcohol despite its illegality. But in fact, the CDC's 2013 Youth Risk Behavior Survey (conducted every other year) found that 35 percent of high school students admitted to drinking alcohol in the preceding thirty days.

Teenagers are faced with many choices—from the decision to smoke or use illegal drugs to taking part in cyberbullying or engaging in sexual relationships. For teens the world suddenly becomes a far more complicated place, with a wide range of choices that often have no easy answers. Drinking is one of the most common issues that require such a choice.

Chapter One

The Faces of Underage Drinking

On July 17, 1984, a special ceremony was held in the White House Rose Garden. President Ronald Reagan had just signed a bill into law that would make it illegal in all fifty states for anyone under age twenty-one to purchase or consume alcohol. It was called the National Minimum Drinking Age Act, and the president was proud of it.

Before the new law was passed, each state had determined its own minimum legal drinking age (MLDA). There were problems with this system, however, because many teens as young as eighteen who lived in a state whose MLDA was twenty-one were driving across state lines to another state where they could drink legally. The result was a skyrocketing number of drunken driving accidents involving teens—a problem that the new bill would presumably solve. As Reagan noted:

> This problem is bigger than the individual States. It's a grave national problem, and it touches all our lives. With the problem so clear-cut and the proven solution at hand, we have no misgiving about this judicious use of Federal power. I'm convinced that it will help persuade State legislators to act in the national interest to save our children's lives, by raising the drinking age to 21 across the country.[4]

The Prevalence of Underage Drinkers

But although the 1984 law banned drinking for anyone under twenty-one, experts note that more than thirty years later, the number of underage drinkers in the United States remains discouragingly high—more than 11 million. Most are teenagers between fourteen and twenty, but a disturbing trend shows that even children as young as eleven are experimenting with alcohol.

According to the website of Caron Treatment Centers, which provides help to those addicted to alcohol and other drugs, 75 percent of twelfth graders, 66 percent of tenth graders, and 40 percent of eighth graders in the United States have consumed alcohol. "With over 10.8 million underage drinkers in the United States," notes the site, "alcohol is the 'drug of choice' for America's youth."[5]

> "This problem is bigger than the individual States. . . . It touches all our lives."[4]
>
> —Ronald Reagan, fortieth US president.

Experts on substance abuse say it is a worrisome trend because many of these underage drinkers are unable to control their use of alcohol. As a result, they can become addicted. In fact, in 2013, an estimated 679,000 adolescents received treatment for an alcohol problem in a specialized facility, such as a treatment center, or an inpatient substance abuse program.

Underage drinking has become an immense problem that is having dangerous and frightening effects on those under age twenty-one. "A third of kids ages 12 to 17 had their first drink before 13," says Susan Foster, director of policy research for Columbia University's National Center on Addiction and Substance Abuse. "That's about 6.4 million kids, many more than there have been historically. Very young drinkers are a huge concern."[6]

Drinking for a Purpose?

Suzanne was one of these very young drinkers. Now fifteen, she admits that she has been drinking since she was eleven years old. She explains that when she was in fifth grade, she began having bouts of anxiety—which she refers to as "scary spells"—and had no idea how to cope with them. She remembers:

I was so freaked out by my spells. I didn't know what they meant. I was really nervous but I didn't know why. I was afraid of being called on in class because I was afraid of saying the wrong answer. I was afraid I wouldn't have anyone to talk to at recess, and afraid that I wouldn't get picked for a team in phys ed class. I was afraid I'd throw up at lunch. It was like I was scared of *everything* all of a sudden, and I don't know why.[7]

Carolyn, one of Suzanne's friends, told her that when her own mother was stressed after a hard day of work or after a fight with her ex-husband, she would make herself a drink to relax. Carolyn suggested that Suzanne try it. After school the

Research reveals that one-third of teen drinkers had their first drink before age thirteen. Drinking at such an early age raises the risk of long-term problems with alcohol and can lead to other difficulties.

girls went to Carolyn's house and experimented with different alcoholic beverages. Suzanne drank a little bit of vodka, which she says tasted awful, but she did feel relaxed afterward.

"So I started doing that every day," she says. "My parents had some liquor in the cupboard, and I started using it. Back then I didn't think of it really as drinking. Carolyn said I should just think of it like taking liquid medicine—like the pink stuff I used to take when I was a little kid and had an ear infection."[8]

Drinking to Escape

Other young drinkers begin using alcohol as a way to take their minds off their personal problems or family issues. This was the reason Ben began to drink; his parents were going through a difficult time in their marriage. He says that for years they had had disagreements and argued occasionally, but this time the conflict was worse than it had ever been.

"Every day was hard," he says. "I didn't even want to be in the house when they were there, but I didn't want to leave if [my younger sister] Katie was around—it really bothered her to hear them fighting. They were either screaming and calling each other names or they were ignoring each other."[9]

Ben says that he used alcohol as an escape. He stayed in his room or retreated to the basement so he did not have to listen to his parents' angry voices. There was a bar in the basement, and one day he had the idea of having a drink. Though he had tried beer, he had never tasted anything stronger. He decided to pour a shot glass full of whiskey and found it was far stronger than he had imagined. But it was worth it, he says, because it helped him tune out the angry voices upstairs—at least temporarily.

> "Carolyn said I should just think of it like taking liquid medicine—like the pink stuff I used to take when I was a little kid and had an ear infection."[8]
>
> —Suzanne, speaking about a past experience with alcohol.

An Early Beginning to a Drinking Problem

Many teens who become drinkers got their start when they were very young. Mary Brennan, who lived in a Chicago suburb, was only ten when she had her first encounter with alcohol. She had gone to a friend's house after school, where the friend's older brother, an eighth grader, was drinking with some of his school friends. The boys were mixing orange juice with vodka—a concoction known as a screwdriver.

She was excited when the boys offered her a drink, later remembering, "I felt like, wow, now I'm one of the older kids." By the time she was twelve, she was binge drinking almost every weekend, occasionally blacking out from the liquor. By age fourteen she had increased her drinking to every day. And by age fifteen she was sneaking vodka into school in Gatorade bottles.

At age sixteen, Mary went to a party, smoked a lot of marijuana, single-handedly drank an entire bottle of vodka, and passed out. When she regained consciousness later, she felt terrible. She begged the others to call an ambulance for help, but nobody was willing to do it, worrying that they might get arrested. "Everything was spinning. I was lying on the floor throwing up. . . . I was convinced I was going to die."

Eventually, one of the partygoers drove Mary home. She felt ill for the rest of the night, but she started drinking again the very next day.

Quoted in Heather Millar, "The Hidden Epidemic of Very Young Alcoholics," WebMD. www.webmd.com.

Boredom and Drinking

Another common reason teens choose to drink is boredom. In 2009 an online survey conducted by Drinkaware, a charitable organization active in the United Kingdom, found that 8 percent of sixteen- and seventeen-year-olds said they drank at least once a week simply because they were bored over the summer months when school was not in session.

More than one thousand of the teens surveyed—61 percent—stated that they intended to drink during the summer. "Young people drink when they're bored, and over the summer holidays this is likely to increase,"[10] notes Chris Sorek, Drinkaware's chief executive. Also discouraging, say experts, is that boredom is cited as the top reason that teens and young adults who have completed treatment programs began drinking again.

"We've seen too many kids who have nothing to do, and no one to hang out with anymore," says one teen counselor. "They haven't developed other activities that interest them like drinking did. And yes, they do have friends, but usually those were their drinking friends. And so it's disappointing, but it's not a shock to see those kids go back to their old ways. They're simply bored, and drinking can take their mind off the boredom for a while."[11]

Fun and Curiosity

Not every underage drinker chooses to drink because of a problem. Many underage drinkers say that they drink not to escape or avoid something uncomfortable, but to have fun, according to substance abuse counselor Dr. Kirsten Dawson. "They do it because they can," she explains. "Simply because they have the opportunity to do it, and they've heard it can be fun and they want to try it. They are interested in knowing what drinking is like, and at the same time, it's a pretty easy way to rebel against established rules."[12]

Sixteen-year-old Piper agrees with Dawson's assessment and admits that for a long time she has wanted to try drinking because she is curious about what being drunk feels like. She explains:

> I started thinking about it back in seventh grade. You hear about kids having fun, losing their inhibitions or whatever. It seems like all of the kids in my school drink. I don't want to drink so much I get sick or dizzy, and I wouldn't make stupid decisions like drinking and driving. I wouldn't do that. But I do think it would be interesting to try it—so if I have an opportunity to do a little experimenting, I guess I'd have to admit that I'm pretty sure I'd do it.[13]

Binge Drinking

One of the most disturbing aspects of teen drinking—no matter what the reason—is the prevalence of binge drinking. The point of binge drinking is not to enjoy the taste of alcohol or the conversation with fellow drinkers or partygoers, but instead to consume a great amount of alcohol very quickly and get drunk. "It's not like when you're older, like, say, in your mid- or late-twenties," explains Marvin Smith, who says he drank far too much when he was in his teens. "By then, you have a beer or a drink with your friends while you're talking about movies you like, or just having conversations like that. But for teenagers, it's all about getting drunk fast, binge drinking just so you can feel that high."[14]

The NIAAA defines binge drinking as consuming enough alcohol to bring a person's blood alcohol concentration (BAC) to .08 or more. For a boy, this is defined as the standard amount of alcohol in five or more mixed drinks, each with approximately 0.6 ounces (18 ml) of alcohol; five 12-ounce (355 ml) beers;

Teenage binge drinkers want to feel the effects of the alcohol right away. So they drink as much as they can as quickly as they can.

or five servings of about 5 ounces (148 ml) of wine. For a girl, binge drinking would require four or more such drinks. For both boys and girls, binge drinking means that this amount of alcohol is drunk in a single sitting—usually defined as a period of one and a half to two hours.

Binge drinking is extremely dangerous because drinking heavily at such a rapid pace can result in acute alcohol poisoning—a potentially deadly condition that occurs when the body cannot break down the alcohol fast enough and it builds up in the bloodstream. Bingeing has become an alarming practice among underage drinkers. In fact, the NIAAA says that as much as 90 percent of the alcohol drunk by those under twenty-one is consumed in the form of binge drinking.

House Drinking Parties

Teen drinking can take place in any number of venues, but the most common are house parties. House parties are often informal, with invitations spread by word of mouth. Frequently these parties involve a variety of drinking games—which can be highly dangerous.

Drinking games encourage binge drinking. In fact, some experts at the University of Michigan Institute for Social Research have cited drinking games as a risk factor for the growing practice known as extreme binge drinking, which is defined as drinking ten or more drinks in a row. In 2013 the researchers announced that 10 percent of high school seniors have engaged in extreme binge drinking, and 5.6 percent say they have consumed as many as fifteen or more drinks in a single sitting. They also found that high school boys were more likely to binge drink (24 percent) than high school girls (15 percent).

One game that encourages binge drinking is Super Power Hour. During one variation of this game, a player must drink a shot glass (1 ounce, or 29.5 ml) of beer every minute for 100 minutes. By the time the 100 minutes are up, the winning player will have drunk 100 ounces (3 L) of beer. If the player is a 170-pound (77 kg) male, his BAC will likely be .17;

a 140-pound (64 kg) female would have .26 BAC. Both BAC readings are well over the legal level for intoxication.

Another popular drinking game is known as Edward Forty Hands, a takeoff on the movie titled *Edward Scissorhands.* To play this game, a participant has a 40-ounce (1.2 L) bottle of malt liquor taped to each hand. The player must drink all 80 ounces (2.4 L) of malt liquor before being able to use his or her hands. According to the website of the substance abuse therapy organization Right Step, "The need to go to the bathroom or to do anything with the hands impels the game player to drink dangerously fast."[15]

A Dangerous Online Drinking Game

One of the most disturbing of the many drinking games popular with teen drinkers is one that takes place not at a drinking party but rather online. It is known as Neknominate or Nek Nominating. It is thought to have begun in 2014 in Australia as a way for drinkers to challenge each other by filming themselves guzzling (known as "necking" or "neking" in Australia and the United Kingdom) an entire pint (473 ml) of alcohol—usually beer—in a risky setting, such as outside a police station.

The drinker then posts the video on social media—most often Facebook or YouTube—and nominates, or challenges, two others to outdo him or her within the next twenty-four hours. Those who are named in the challenge must drink a greater amount than the challenger drank, drink it more quickly, or drink it in a more unusual or riskier setting. Anyone who is challenged and refuses is ridiculed mercilessly online.

The challenges almost always become more and more outlandish. For instance, one teen outdid his challenger by drinking a large amount of vodka from a toilet as friends dangled him upside down by his ankles. Another teen mixed his drink with a dead mouse and a bit of mouthwash. One seventeen-year-old girl responded to a Neknominate challenge by crushing moths and roaches and adding them to a glass of whiskey. She then stood on a table and downed the mixture as pub onlookers

17

recorded the feat and cheered when she smacked her lips as though the beverage had tasted delicious.

Not surprisingly, health professionals are troubled by the widespread popularity of what they view as a dangerous phenomenon. As of January 2015 at least five young people had died from accepting challenges via Neknominate. "This is a lethal game," warns Dr. Sarah Jarvis, the medical advisor for Drinkaware. "The point about alcohol is that it affects your ability to recognize that you're in danger, and it absolutely affects your ability to react to danger. So we have a double whammy."[16]

Solitary Teen Drinkers

Not all underage drinking takes place in the company of others. In fact, a recent study by researchers conducted at the Pittsburgh Adolescent Alcohol Research Center found that a surprising number of teens prefer to drink alone. The research team interviewed 709 adolescents between the ages of twelve and eighteen and asked them about their use of alcohol in the past twelve months.

The researchers learned that teens who drink alone are far more likely to have alcohol problems and tend to be heavier drinkers than those who drink in group settings. The solitary drinkers also are more likely to drink as a result of negative emotions. Finally, those who drink alone are far more likely to develop problems with alcohol in adulthood than those who drink mostly at parties and other social events.

Tammy Chung, an associate professor of psychiatry and epidemiology at the University of Pittsburgh School of Medicine, is a coauthor of the study. She says that the findings are quite troublesome: "Because adolescent solitary drinking is an early warning sign for alcohol use disorder in young adulthood, and solitary drinking tends to occur in response to negative emotions, youth who report solitary drinking might benefit from interventions that teach more adaptive strategies for coping with negative emotions."[17]

Dangers for Teen Drinkers

With many teens and even preteens choosing to drink, society in general has many concerns about the potential dangers of underage drinking. Underage drinking can have extremely dangerous consequences—and not only to the drinkers themselves. Teens who drink, for example, are often involved in automobile accidents because they drive under the influence.

The Youth Risk Behavior Survey monitors teen behaviors such as risky sexual practices and illicit drug use as well as the use of alcohol and tobacco. In 2013 (the most recent survey) high school students were asked whether in the past thirty days they had driven after drinking or had ridden with a driver

Las Vegas police investigate the scene of a fatal crash involving a suspected drunk driver. The outcome is rarely good when teens drink and drive.

The Dangers of Teen Drunk Driving

In 2014 Cindy and Brian Hoeflinger of Elyria, Ohio, made a short video. It was a montage much like the ones parents put together to show at a happy event like a high school graduation party or a wedding. But this montage, featuring their son, Brian Jr., practicing his golf swing and goofing around with his siblings and friends, was meant for an assembly at Elyria Catholic High School. The ending of the video showed their son's car tangled into a ruined pile of metal and right next to it, the tree that Brian had struck. Their son had died in the crash.

"Nobody plans to die," Brian's father told the students. "You don't go to a party with your friends and say, 'I'm going to die tonight. I'm not going to make it back home.' But that is exactly what happened to my son. He got drunk at a party, he drove his car home from a party, and he died."

The Hoeflingers reminded the students of the chilling statistics of teen drinking, including the facts that one in five teens binge drink and 62 percent of all high school seniors have been drunk. One senior at the assembly noted, "I think it opened a lot of kids' eyes out there and let them know they are not invincible."

Quoted in Lisa Robertson, "Parents Share Story of Son's Death in Drunken Driving Crash," *Elyria (OH) Chronicle-Telegram*, October 2, 2014. http://chronicle.northcoastnow.com.

who had been drinking alcohol. Ten percent admitted to driving after drinking, and 22 percent said they had ridden with a driver who had been drinking.

Lloyd Mueller, a retired St. Paul, Minnesota, restaurant worker, experienced the effects of teen drinking and driving firsthand. In October 2012 Mueller was hit by a sixteen-year-old driver who was under the influence. "The boy was hurt worse than me," he says:

He had a bad concussion and a lot of cuts and bruises. I had a banged-up knee, and that was about it. He got out of his car, and didn't seem coherent. The police arrived and did a breathalyzer on him, and [it registered] over a .24, which is three times the BAC necessary to be cited for DUI [driving under the influence]. I guess with that BAC, both of us should be grateful to be alive. My friends asked me, "Weren't you furious?" But I have a grandson almost his age, and I felt bad for both of us.[18]

Addiction and Health Concerns

One of the most frightening outcomes when teens choose to drink is that they may become alcohol dependent—addicted to alcohol. In fact, according to the National Council on Alcoholism and Drug Dependence, those who have their first drink before age fifteen are more than four times more likely to develop alcohol dependence than those who do not try alcohol until they reach the legal drinking age.

Cole Rucker, the founder and chief executive officer of a California treatment center called Echo Malibu, agrees that the number of younger drinkers is on the rise. "We've received calls from parents of kids as young as 8," he says. "Every year, alcohol use shows up in younger and younger kids."[19]

Teen drinkers are also at risk of experiencing health problems—some of which are potentially life threatening. One of the most dangerous is alcohol poisoning, a consequence of binge drinking. Too much alcohol in a short time raises the BAC to dangerous levels, and that can affect a person's breathing, heart rate, and body temperature—which can lead to coma and death.

One of the most shocking health issues is a disease that was once seen mostly in middle-aged men who had been binge drinking for decades. Known as cirrhosis of the liver, the condition frequently develops over years of heavy drinking. But today doctors are diagnosing cirrhosis of the liver in young women and men in their late teens and early twenties.

"What we know is that 30 years ago it was very unusual to see someone in their twenties with liver cirrhosis," says expert

Andrew Langford of the British Liver Trust. "Now it is quite common for [hospital] liver units to have young people in their twenties dying of liver disease because they started drinking so early."[20]

The issue of teenage drinking has become a concern not only for the families of underage drinkers, but also for society as a whole. "Our communities thrive when people are productive, happy, and healthy," says Marvin Smith, who now speaks to groups of young men who are trying to stop drinking. "We can't afford to ignore or write off any of our young people who are struggling with alcohol. The idea of letting them slide further into alcoholism is simply appalling."[21]

Chapter Two

Factors That Influence Underage Drinking

As the number of teen drinkers grows, parents, teachers, counselors, and even law enforcement agencies are trying to identify and understand the factors that are influencing these teens—and even some preteens—to drink. Some of these factors are quite surprising, whereas others—such as the strong influence of peer pressure—are very predictable.

The Power of Peer Pressure

Pressure from one's friends or classmates is an incredibly powerful force. Peer pressure can cause teens to adopt certain types of behaviors—from what sorts of clothing they wear, which friends they choose, and even whether they elect to drink or smoke. An activity such as drinking may seem wrong to some of the individuals in a group, yet the pressure on young people to do what the group is doing can overwhelm an individual's better judgment. Not surprisingly, when it comes to underage drinking, according to a study by the NIAAA, "evidence suggests that the most reliable predictor of a youth's drinking behavior is the drinking behavior of his or her friends."[22]

Allie is a seventeen-year-old high school student who lives in a Chicago suburb and is well aware of the power of peer pressure. When she was in eighth grade, she started hanging out with her friends after school at the home of a girl whose parents were not home. With little to do, the girls eventually started to experiment with alcohol. "At first different things— mostly wine and beer at first, because that's mostly what

Corey's parents had in their bar in the basement," says Allie. "But then the girls got braver and started bringing in liquor from home and making mixed drinks."[23]

Stronger than Promises

Allie says that she did not participate in the drinking at first, for two reasons. One was that she had just completed a unit in her health class about the dangers of drinking alcohol, and much of what she had learned was still fresh in her mind. She had no intention of becoming addicted to alcohol or of losing memory or brain cells because of underage drinking. The second reason she did not drink with her friends right away was because her parents had talked with her about not drinking until she was twenty-one. "I gave them my word that I would wait," she says. "And I'd never really lied to my parents before, so I didn't want to break my word."[24]

> "Evidence suggests that the most reliable predictor of a youth's drinking behavior is the drinking behavior of his or her friends."[22]
>
> —National Institute on Alcohol Abuse and Alcoholism.

But although she had good intentions, at one point Allie realized that she wanted to drink, just as the other girls were doing. "I was the only one who wasn't actually drinking, and I felt weird, like they were looking at me wondering why I wasn't drinking, too. I think that was the moment I realized how strong peer pressure could be—I knew it was wrong, but I also knew I wouldn't be part of [this group] if I kept refusing to try it."[25]

Though Allie did not intend to drink, she eventually made the choice to do it anyway. She was eager to be part of the group, and having her peers like her was very important to her—even more important, in that moment, than keeping a promise she had made to her parents. Youth counselor Elizabeth Berg says:

It happens all the time. To be seen as different from one's peers is difficult for most teens, because they want to be accepted and valued by their classmates and friends.

Even if doing what their friends are doing seems wrong to them, they may go along just so they aren't perceived as different. And that's the moment parents ask the eternal question after their teen has done something stupid because of peer pressure—"So if your friends were all jumping off a cliff, would you do it, too?" My own parents asked me the same thing, and my parents' parents probably asked them that, too.[26]

Parental Influence

But peer pressure does not explain all underage drinking. Parents, too, can be a strong influence in whether a young person decides to drink. Paul Sjorensen, a former sobriety counselor who has worked with chemically dependent teens, says that

"Binge in a Can"

A 2011 letter, signed by seventeen attorneys general and one city attorney, asks Pabst Brewing Company to make changes in a product marketed as a "binge in a can." A single can of Blast, a high-octane flavored malt beverage, has the alcohol content of nearly five servings of alcohol. According to the CDC, anyone who consumes one 23.5-ounce (666 g) can of Blast within an hour will have engaged in binge drinking—probably without realizing it. The letter stated, "We believe the manufacture and marketing of this flavored 'binge in a can' poses a grave public safety threat."

The letter criticized the company for a marketing campaign that is likely to attract underage drinkers. Among the concerns: Blast flavors such as strawberry lemonade, blueberry pomegranate, and grape are likely to appeal to teens; the product spokesperson, rap star Snoop Dogg, also has teen appeal; and the company has advertised Blast on social media sites frequented by teens. The letter signers urged the company to reduce the number of servings of alcohol in a single can and to ensure that product marketing does not target underage youth.

Letter to Charles Dean Metropoulos, Chairman and CEO, Pabst Brewing Company, "Blast by Colt 45," April 21, 2011. www.tn.gov/attorneygeneral/cases/pabst/pabst.pdf.

Parental behaviors can influence youth behavior. Research suggests that teens who see a parent drunk are more likely to also drink—and get drunk.

long before they are old enough even to think about drinking, children learn how to deal with alcohol by watching their own parents. He explains:

> If Mom or Dad comes home from work and the first thing they do is have a beer or a cocktail, they're modeling behavior that says, "I've been waiting for this all day," or "This relaxes me after a tough day." Or if they get some unexpected good news, some parents may have a drink to celebrate. And to their children, that behavior seems valid, and so later, when that child gets a bit older and feels stressed out from school, or when a celebration is in order, having a drink with their friends can seem like a logical, grown-up thing to do.[27]

One very strong influence on teens is witnessing their parents drinking to the point of intoxication. A research project conducted by the National Center on Addiction and Substance Abuse at Columbia University (CASA) found that teens who have seen one or both parents drunk are more likely to get drunk than teens who have not.

Tacit Approval

Parents may convey a pro-drinking message to their children in less obvious ways as well, sometimes when the child is quite young. Rather than explaining to his children that drinking is only for grown-ups, for example, a father might find it cute when his son sings along with the beer commercial on television or asks to have a sip of Daddy's beer. The father does not say outright that drinking is a fun activity, nor does he urge the child to drink, but simply the fact that he is rewarding the child with attention is giving tacit, or unspoken, approval.

When children become older, parents can also tacitly influence their teen's choice to drink if they are not clear or firm about their expectations. In 2014 a national organization called Mothers Against Drunk Driving (MADD) released the results of an online survey of 663 high school students. Only 8 percent of the participants whose parents had clearly communicated that they considered underage drinking to be totally unacceptable were likely to drink. By contrast, 42 percent of teens whose parents believed underage drinking was somewhat unacceptable, somewhat acceptable, or completely acceptable were apt to drink.

> "It's undeniable the influence parents have on their teens' behavior."[28]
>
> —MADD president Jan Withers.

A CASA survey found that fathers are especially influential in whether a teen drinks. Adolescents who believe their father is ambivalent about their drinking alcoholic beverages are 2.5 times more likely to get drunk than those teens whose father clearly disapproves of their drinking.

"It's undeniable the influence parents have on their teens' behavior," said MADD national president Jan Withers in a news release. "Our kids are listening; but what parents say and how they say it makes all the difference."[28]

Message Received?

That was the case with nineteen-year-old Justin, a college student from St. Paul, Minnesota. Justin says when he was just three or four years old, his father would let him sit on his lap while he watched TV and drank beer.

"He gave me little sips of his beer, and he laughed when I told him I liked the taste," Justin recalls. "He even bought me a little red t-shirt with the letters DDB on it. He said it stood for 'Daddy's Drinking Buddy,' though I know now that my mom really didn't approve of the shirt. But I definitely got the message when I was pretty little that it was a guy thing Dad and I did together, and that he thought it was kind of cool."[29]

Greg, also a nineteen-year-old college student, says that when he was in high school, his parents communicated highly contradictory messages about drinking to him and his friends. On the one hand, his parents would not let him go to parties where they suspected liquor might be available. On the other hand, they routinely permitted Greg and his friends to drink in their home.

> "[My father] gave me little sips of his beer [when I was four], and he laughed when I told him I liked the taste."[29]
>
> —Justin, age nineteen.

According to Greg, he was not allowed to go anywhere if teens might be driving after drinking. But even when Greg was seventeen and eighteen, his parents allowed him and his friends to drink beer as long as they stayed in the house. They were forbidden to drive or roam around, and as a precaution, his parents took the boys' car keys so they could not get in an accident or get pulled over for a DUI.

Greg insists that his parents were not outwardly encouraging him or his friends to drink, nor were they supplying the beer. "They were just making sure that if and when we did drink, we wouldn't present a danger to ourselves or to other people. But in a way, they were sort of okaying our underage drinking. I don't know what else you could call it."[30]

Movies and Alcohol

Many psychologists have wondered whether teens who have watched scenes of alcohol drinking in movies are more likely to use alcohol themselves, even though they are underage. Claire McCarthy of Harvard Medical School decided to find out and published her findings in the April 2015 issue of the journal *Pediatrics.*

McCarthy randomly selected fifty current movies and categorized them according to how many minutes in each depicted alcohol consumption. She and her assistants then asked her subjects—five thousand British fifteen-year-olds—which of the films they had seen and whether they had done any binge drinking. She also asked them about their family habits and socioeconomic status. Approximately half of the teens admitted to having taken part in binge drinking, and 86 percent said they had already tried alcohol.

Significantly, those who had watched the most minutes of onscreen alcohol use were 25 percent more likely to have tried alcohol than those who had had the least exposure. And those teens who watched the most movies with alcohol scenes were 75 percent more likely to binge drink and were twice as likely to drink weekly or have problems that were related to drinking.

Bombarded by Alcohol Advertising

In addition to parental attitudes, another force that has been cited as influencing underage drinking is the ever-growing number of beer and wine television commercials to which teens are constantly exposed. Hundreds of millions of dollars are spent on advertising each year by companies that produce alcoholic beverages, and critics argue that those ads are often aimed at children and teens, even though young people cannot legally purchase or drink such products until they are twenty-one.

These critics point to the fact that many of those commercials air during television shows that have a large teenage audience. This is nothing new, say experts; a few years ago the *American Journal of Public Health* published a survey showing a striking correlation between the numbers of a show's teen viewers and the frequency of alcohol advertising on cable television stations. William Lowe, who has done research on the alcohol and tobacco industries in the United States, explains the reasoning behind such advertising: "[Companies] target teenagers because they want to build up loyalty to a brand. They want to get teenagers and even pre-teens on board, and even though they're too young to buy beer or liquor, they're old enough to notice the brand name on a race car, or to buy a hat or sweatshirt with 'Budweiser' or 'Jack Daniels' on it."[31]

A race car belonging to driver Dale Earnhardt Jr. sports the Budweiser logo. Studies show that exposure to advertising like this increases the likelihood of teens experimenting with alcohol.

Unfortunately, the strategy seems to be working. Studies have suggested that young people's exposure to alcohol ads increases the likelihood that they will begin drinking before they are of legal age—and influences them to increase their alcoholic intake still more if they have already begun drinking. Moreover, data from 2012 shows that for each dollar the alcohol industry spends on youth advertising, young people drink 3 percent more each month.

Getting the Message Through Music

In addition to ads and commercials on radio and television, music is another source of teen exposure to alcohol-related content. According to a study conducted by the University of Pittsburgh School of Medicine, the lyrics of rhythm and blues, rap, rock, and hip-hop music all frequently mention alcohol brand names. Too, say researchers, the various brands are often "associated with a luxury lifestyle, characterized by degrading sexual activity, wealth, partying, violence, and the use of drugs."[32]

The University of Pittsburgh researchers analyzed nearly eight hundred of the songs most popular among teens between 2005 and 2007 and found that in 25 percent of them, a brand name of alcohol was mentioned. That means that each hour, listeners heard about 3.4 brand references—and most of those references were far more positive than negative. Since the average teen is exposed to 2.5 hours of popular music every day, the study estimated that each year "the average adolescent is exposed to about 3,000 references to alcoholic brands while listening to music."[33]

Country Music's Drinkin' Lyrics

Lyrics about drinking and alcohol have always been features of country music. Merle Haggard's "Misery and Gin" and the George Jones classic "If Drinkin' Don't Kill Me (Her Memory Will)" are examples from the past. In many of those songs, the narrator is drinking to forget a painful breakup or other sad experience.

In contrast, many twenty-first-century country singers depict drinking not as a means to cope, but as a way to have fun. Tim McGraw's "Meanwhile Back at Mama's" tells the listener there are two twelve-packs in the title character's fridge. The second verse of Dustin Lynch's "Where It's At (Yep, Yep)" includes a hip reference to Pabst Blue Ribbon beer and suggestive lyrics—from poppin' tops to rockin' all night.

Many of these songs come out of songwriting "factories," groups of staff writers. Naturally, they push ideas that will sell—and it appears that mentioning drinking is a winner. In 2013 three of sixty songs on the Hot Country Songs chart mentioned alcohol in the title of the song. The next year there were seven on the list. One does not have to guess where "Drunk on a Plane" is going, or what "Sunshine and Whiskey" offers the listener. According to Nashville music executive Jon Loba, "A year ago it seemed like 75 percent of the songs that were pitched had some kind of bro-country, drinking, party theme to it."[34]

But there is some evidence that the trend might be getting old. In July 2014 eight of the top ten country records had some reference to drinking, and when a Rhode Island radio station asked listeners what they would like to tell Nashville, one common theme came back: What is up with all the drinking songs?

Marketing Alcohol with Teens in Mind

Teens who are not influenced to drink by alcohol advertising or musical references may nonetheless be tempted by a type of alcoholic beverage that critics say is designed to be particularly appealing to an underage market. Often referred to derisively as "alcopops"—a slang term that is a combination of *alcohol* and *soda pop*—the drinks are ready-mixed combinations of beer, wine, or a liquor such as vodka and a very sweet, fruity base. They can contain as much as two or three times the level of alcohol in a can of beer, but because of their sweetness, the liquor taste is not as overwhelming as it is in other alcoholic beverages.

On the shelves of a liquor store cooler, alcopops bear a striking resemblance to energy drinks, with eye-catching labels in vivid blue, green, red, and yellow. With interesting names like Sparks, Joose, and Kiss Mix, they are geared to appeal especially to female teens who may not like the taste of alcohol but who are eager to feel the buzz from an alcoholic drink.

Tracy, a seventeen-year-old Wisconsin high school junior, admits that she enjoys drinking several brands of alcopops, but especially Four Loko. "I'm kind of ashamed to admit that I've kind of become addicted to them—especially the watermelon flavor," she says. "They don't have that overpowering liquor taste, you know? But you mostly get the buzz, because one can is the equivalent of like five drinks. Practically everybody I know loves them."[35]

The Teenage Brain

Although there are many external factors that can influence underage drinking, it is an internal force—the teenage brain—that bears a great deal of the blame. The brain of a teenager is not yet completely formed, and as a result, important neurological functions are not yet operational, such as making informed decisions or foreseeing possible dangers or other problems before they occur.

For many years scientists believed that the brain, which reaches about 95 percent of its adult size by the time a child is around ten years old, was nearly fully developed at this age as well. However, because of the invention of sensitive instruments and procedures such as magnetic resonance imaging, researchers have learned that this is not the case. Critical changes occur within the brain between ages ten and twenty-five; in fact, those changes are so important that many psychologists believe that twenty-five should be the cut-off point for adolescence, rather than the more commonly cited eighteen or twenty-one.

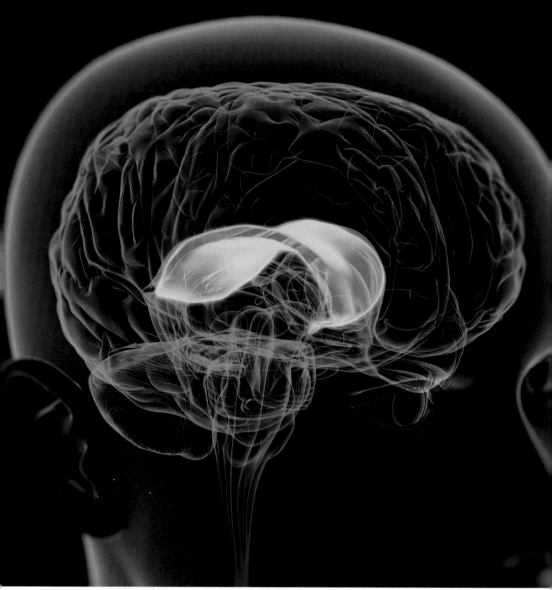

The corpus callosum (yellow-orange in this computer illustration) enables communication between the two hemispheres of the human brain. In teenagers, this and other parts of the brain are still developing—which explains why teens sometimes have difficulty making good choices.

"We used to think that the brain was fully developed by very early teenagerhood and we now realize that the brain doesn't stop developing until mid-20s or even early 30s," says clinical psychologist Sarah Helps. "There's a lot more information and evidence to suggest that actually brain development in various forms goes on throughout the life span."[36]

The Necessity of Myelin

Some of this development occurs deep in the wiring of the corpus callosum, which connects the two halves of the brain, the right and left hemispheres, and allows them to communicate effectively with one another. Until this wiring is complete, the brain's frontal lobe—the part that decides whether something is a good idea or is instead too dangerous or risky—is limited in its ability to make smart, timely decisions.

Pediatric neurologist Frances Jensen stresses that although it may sometimes seem that the frontal lobes of young people between ages twelve and twenty-five are missing, in fact the frontal lobes simply are not completely wired yet. "It's not that [those between twelve and twenty-five] don't have a frontal lobe. And they can use it. But they're going to access it more slowly."[37]

The factor that limits the communication between the two hemispheres in a teenage brain is the lack of myelin, a fatty white coating that insulates the axons, the long nerve fibers of the brain. Coated with myelin, the axons can communicate very well; however, without it the frontal lobe is sluggish, and messages are transmitted neither quickly nor reliably. That means, for example, a teen may decide to drink alcohol and then drive or may shrug off the fact that a friend is drunk and decide to ride with him or her anyway—simply because the halves of the teen's brain are not communicating effectively.

> "We used to think that the brain was fully developed by very early teenagerhood and we now realize that the brain doesn't stop developing until mid-20s or even early 30s."[36]
>
> —Clinical psychologist Sarah Helps.

An Explanation for Teen Behavior

Understanding a teen's brain development can help explain some of these worrisome aspects of teenage behavior, says Pradeep Bhide, a neuroscientist at Florida State University College of Medicine. Still, Bhide emphasizes that it is not only the teens who are affected by decisions made by their not-quite-fully-finished brains: "Psychologists, psychiatrists, educators, neuroscientists, criminal justice professionals, and parents are engaged in a daily struggle to understand and solve the enigma of teenage risky behaviors. Such behaviors impact not only the teenagers who obviously put themselves at serious and lasting risk but also families and societies in general."[38]

By adding the power of peer pressure, frequent cultural references, and powerful marketing campaigns for alcohol to teenagers' unfinished brains, it is not difficult to see why many make the choice to drink despite its dangers.

Chapter Three

What Are the Consequences of Underage Drinking?

The choice to drink alcohol when one is underage is fraught with dangers. From experiencing a higher risk of becoming the victim of a sexual assault, to engaging in behavior that could result in a physical altercation, to becoming physically ill or even sustaining brain damage, teenagers are making a risky decision when they choose to drink.

Binge Drinking

One of the most startling statistics regarding teen drinking, say experts, is that although underage drinkers drink less often than adults, they consume a whopping 11 percent of the alcohol consumed in the United States. The reason, says the NIAAA, is that when they do drink, they tend to drink more than adults.

Approximately 90 percent of young people consume more than 90 percent of their alcohol through binge drinking. Counselor Ellie Adams says:

> The idea of binge drinking has absolutely nothing to do with enjoying the social experience of having a drink with friends, nor is it something that helps one appreciate the taste of the alcoholic beverages. It's actually just a fast track towards one goal: to get very, very drunk—very, very quickly. It's an incredibly dangerous thing to do, but binge drinking is all too common with teenage drinkers. They have little or no experience with the powerful and

potentially deadly effects of alcohol, and that is highly alarming. So combining a teenage drinker with all that alcohol in a very short time? It's a recipe for disaster.[39]

Many teens—as well as many adults—have no idea that consuming a large amount of alcohol in a short amount of time can be so dangerous. The risks largely stem from the way the human body processes alcohol.

Blood Alcohol Levels

From the first sip of a drink, the body begins to absorb the alcohol into the bloodstream. The heart rate speeds up, the skin warms, the blood flow increases, and brain cells speed up the transmission of nerve impulses. It is a pleasant feeling for the drinker, because the alcohol relaxes the body and makes the drinker feel more content. The alcohol also makes the drinker feel happy, because it increases the levels of dopamine, a chemical that affects the brain's pleasure center.

The amount of alcohol in a drinker's bloodstream is responsible for how intoxicated he or she becomes. The BAC, the level of the blood alcohol concentration, provides information on how much the person has drunk. In all fifty US states, for example, the measure of a person being legally drunk is a BAC of .08, meaning he or she has eight parts alcohol for every 1,000 parts of blood. A person with that BAC level is impaired to the extent that muscle control, motor skills, vision, and depth perception are severely compromised—and this impairment is what makes drunk driving so perilous.

> "[Binge drinking is] actually just a fast track towards one goal: to get very, very drunk—very, very quickly."[39]
>
> —Counselor Ellie Adams.

But even before a drinker's BAC reaches the level of .08, alcohol produces noticeable effects. For example, at a BAC of .05, a drinker's judgment is not functioning at its best. He

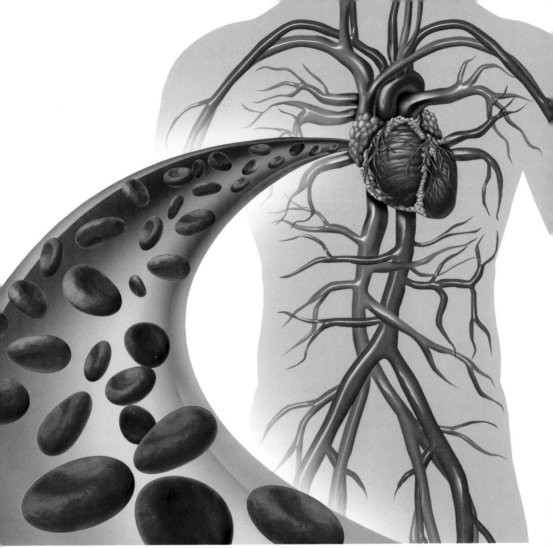

In the human circulatory system (pictured), blood carries oxygen and nutrients throughout the body. Alcohol also goes directly into the bloodstream.

or she is less capable of making rational decisions—and as a result, the person might decide to drive or to ride with a driver who has been drinking.

The human body does not process alcohol quickly. In fact, it takes about an hour for it to process one drink. So if someone is binge drinking, it is likely that he or she is drinking far more quickly than the body can break down the alcohol. The large amount of alcohol in the body acts like a poison, stopping the body's systems from working properly—and that can have deadly consequences.

Alcohol Poisoning

That is what happened to sixteen-year-old Julia Gonzalez in December 2007. She left home with friends at about 7:00 p.m., and the next morning at 5:00 a.m., her body was spotted by a passerby in a park in Turlock, California. Though the circumstances that led to her death were not known, the coroner performed an autopsy, including a toxicology screen—tests to see if there were chemicals such as alcohol or other drugs in Gonzalez's system that may have played a role in her death.

When the toxicology report came back, it supplied the answer of how Gonzalez died. Her BAC was an almost unbelievable .52, more than six times the level for an adult to be considered legally drunk. As deputy coroner Kristi Herr Ah You explained to reporters, Gonzalez would have had to drink a great deal of alcohol in a very short time to have a BAC at that level.

"At 5 feet 2 inches tall and about 100 pounds, Julia would have had to drink the equivalent of one pint of 86-proof whiskey in an hour to register that high," she said. "We're not saying that's what she drank, but that's what you'd have to drink at that weight to get to that level."[40]

Herr Ah You believes that Gonzalez's friends had abandoned her when she began to show signs of alcohol poisoning—likely including confusion, vomiting, seizures, and losing consciousness. And because no one was there to call for help once she became unconscious, she died.

More Dangerous for Women

Although binge drinking can be extremely risky for anyone, it is particularly dangerous for women. Because physically the female body is not capable of processing alcohol as quickly as the male body, the alcohol remains in a female's system longer. This puts her in far more danger for problems resulting from the buildup of alcohol in her bloodstream. And according to a 2012 report from the CDC, one in eight women in the United States participates in binge drinking. Among high school girls, the number is far higher—one in five.

Taylor Anderson, the associate director of Drexel University's Behavioral Healthcare Education division, says that young women who binge drink are facing serious consequences. "Women tend to feel the effects of alcohol quicker than men—on average, after two drinks. Alcohol affects the brain. Once you feel the effects of alcohol, one more drink might seem like a good idea, when it hadn't when you started drinking. It lowers your inhibitions, which puts you at greater danger for [engaging in] dangerous situations."[41]

Being Drunk and a Victim

One such danger is the risk of becoming a victim of sexual assault, as revealed in a 2012 study by the University of Georgia. Published in the journal *Violence and Victims*, the study found that female freshmen college students who drank four or more alcoholic beverages in one day at the start of the study were 33 percent more likely to be sexually assaulted in the following months. In comparison, women who drank four alcoholic beverages in two days or more were 17 percent more likely to be sexually assaulted. Only 6 percent of the nondrinkers experienced a sexual assault over the course of the study.

The sexual victimization of underage female drinkers is not limited to college students. In Saratoga, California, in 2012, three teenage boys sexually assaulted Audrie Pott, a fifteen-year-old Saratoga High School student, by digitally penetrating her. The assault occurred when she was passed out drunk at a party after consuming cocktails made of vodka and Gatorade. When she woke up, Pott found that her clothes had been taken off, and her assailants had used Sharpie markers to write demeaning and humiliating messages all over her her body. Pott told authorities that she had no

> "Alcohol affects the brain. Once you feel the effects . . . one more drink might seem like a good idea, when it hadn't when you started drinking."[41]
>
> —Taylor Anderson, associate director of Drexel University's Behavioral Healthcare Education division.

Audrie Pott, pictured in a photograph behind her mother, committed suicide in 2012. Audrie was sexually assaulted by three boys after she got drunk and passed out at a party. The boys had used a Sharpie to write on her naked body; photos then circulated online.

memory of the incident. According to the sheriff's report, there was "writing on her breast that '[the name of a boy who was at the party] was here'—and the drawing of arrows and circles and other scribbles all over her body and close to her genitalia.'"[42]

Not surprisingly, Pott was devastated and embarrassed—even more so when photographs of her after the assault were posted online for the whole school to see. Shamed and humiliated by the cyberbullying, Pott wrote on Facebook, "My life is ruined. I can't do anything to fix it. I just want this to go away. My life is over. The people I thought I could trust f_____ed me over and then tried to lie to cover it up. I have a reputation for a night I don't even remember and the whole school knows."[43]

Soon afterward, in September 2012, Pott committed suicide, hanging herself at her mother's home. Three boys between fifteen and sixteen admitted to the assault and were arrested but, because they were minors, were sentenced to only thirty days in jail, which they could serve on weekends. Almost three years later, in April 2015, one of the boys publicly apologized to Pott's parents through the local newspaper. "[Audrie] was a great person who didn't deserve anything that happened to her due to my actions," he said. "I apologize. I wish I could make it right."[44]

Poor Decision Making

Another danger that can come from underage drinking is the almost inevitable tendency to make poor decisions while under the influence of alcohol. One extremely dangerous decision—made far too often—is for an underage drinker to get behind the wheel of an automobile or to ride with someone who has been drinking. In 2012 the National Highway Traffic Safety Administration estimated that 24 percent of the young drivers involved in fatal crashes were underage drinkers. That percentage amounts to 926 drivers between ages fifteen and twenty.

> "My life is ruined. I can't do anything to fix it. I just want this to go away."[43]
>
> —Facebook posting by fifteen-year-old Audrie Pott.

This was the scenario in 2006 when two eighteen-year-old Florida college students, Jessica Rasdall and Laura Gorman, spent the night drinking shots and dancing at a popular club. Although both were drunk, Rasdall decided to drive them home. On the way home, she lost control of the car and crashed into a tree. Rasdall was seriously injured, and Gorman was killed instantly—a horror Rasdall has lived with ever since.

Steven, a nineteen-year-old college student, is lucky that his decision to drink and drive did not have such horrific consequences. He lost his driving privileges because of a drunk driving arrest in 2014. He admits that he was well aware of the dangers of drinking and driving, but he made the choice to drive home after partying with friends at a neighborhood bar. Though he says he is furious with himself for making such a stupid decision, he is relieved that he did not harm anyone while driving drunk. Steven insists that the experience taught him a valuable lesson:

> One of the things about alcohol is that it makes you feel confident, relaxed, and capable. But that's a false impression, because you're anything but capable, and you should be anything but confident. And so one part of your brain gives you the message, "You've had a few drinks, and you should call a cab, or give up the keys to let someone else drive," while the other part of your brain says, "Hey, you can handle it—it's just a few miles home. Just go slow." That night I got arrested, I listened to the wrong part of my brain, and that's what got me in trouble. I could have killed somebody, or myself. It was a stupid, childish mistake that I won't make again.[45]

Fighting and Aggression

Another consequence of underage drinking is a lack of inhibition when confronted with a contentious situation. Instead of attempting to work out a conflict by discussing it, for example, it is common for a young drinker to become aggressive and pick a fight. Darren, now thirty-two, admits that he drank in his teens and took part in many arguments that escalated into physical fights:

> It was just what you did. You're at a party and somebody says something, and you shove him or say something back, and then one of the two of you throws a punch, and it just kind of speeds up from there. Lots of times, twenty minutes later, you don't have a clue what the fight was about, that's what was so damned ridiculous about it. Just a lot of testosterone and a lot of posturing, I guess.[46]

According to Professor Mary McMurran of the University of Nottingham in England, fighting and other aggressive behav-

Eyeball Drinking

One of the most changeable aspects of underage drinking seems to be the ongoing challenge to make the experience of getting drunk more intense. Perhaps the oddest of these is consuming hard liquor such as vodka by squirting it directly into one's eye. "Vodka eyeballing," as it is often known among student drinkers, became the rage in Britain and the United States after waitresses in Las Vegas began doing it as a trick to get tips. Within months, YouTube featured more than eight hundred clips of young drinkers pouring vodka into their eyes and seemingly enjoying the instant high.

One nineteen-year-old English woman who tried vodka eyeballing is Melissa, who played on her university's rugby team. She clearly remembers pulling apart her eyelids and letting fellow drinkers in the bar pour a shot of vodka into her left eye. But she has not recovered in the three years since.

Now twenty-two, Melissa is in constant pain. Her left eye constantly waters and has been scarred permanently by the vodka. Even more frightening, doctors have warned her that her eyesight may get worse as she gets older. Clearly, she says, it was a mistake in judgment that she would definitely warn others about trying. "The student drinking culture has gotten completely out of hand and I know because I saw it," she says. "I regarded myself as a normal, sensible teenager, but I got pulled into it myself."

Quoted in Barbara Davies, "'Drinking' Neat Vodka Through Your EYE for a Quick Buzz? It Sounds Insane, but Countless Young People Are Risking Their Sight in This New Craze," *Daily Mail* (London), May 14, 2010. www .dailymail.co.uk.

iors are so much a part of drinking because alcohol reduces one's ability to think straight in a number of ways. "It narrows our focus of attention and gives us tunnel vision," she says. "If someone provokes us while we're drunk, we don't take other factors into account, such as the consequences of rising to the bait. This can lead to violent reactions from people who would usually shrug things off."[47] McMurran adds that alcohol reduces a drinker's level of anxiety—which can be a pleasant feeling. However, sometimes anxiety is a good thing, because it serves to warn people to avoid or escape potentially dangerous or confrontational situations.

Finally, when people drink, they tend to be more likely to misunderstand other people's behavior, perhaps thinking someone is insulting them when no insult is intended. This kind of misunderstanding can quickly escalate into a fistfight or worse, simply because alcohol has muddled one's understanding of an insignificant comment or even a facial expression.

Although experts say that arguments or fights can occur between drinkers of any age, they tend to be far more common in younger drinkers. "A teenager who's been drinking beer with his friends and feels that he's been disrespected doesn't have the emotional brakes to de-escalate a situation," says counselor Ellie Adams. "He is more uninhibited, and more than willing to engage in a loud argument or even a fistfight, just to display his toughness to others."[48]

The Physical Risks of Underage Drinking

Many physicians have long been concerned that underage drinkers may be especially at risk for a number of physical problems—especially because they are far more likely to binge drink. For instance, alcohol can slow down breathing and cause irregular heart rhythms, which can lead to a coma or even death. This tends to be more common in teens than in people over age twenty-one.

Another potentially lethal problem is that after drinking too much, it is common for a drinker to vomit as the body instinctively tries to rid itself of the alcohol. However, heavy drinking affects the gag reflex, which when functioning properly prevents a person from choking. If this occurs, drinkers can choke to death on their own vomit.

Underage drinkers are also at a much higher risk than nondrinkers of developing cirrhosis of the liver—a potentially fatal condition that cannot be reversed. The liver is a vitally important organ that helps rid the body of harmful toxins, cleans the blood, and also processes nutrients that are key to the body's well-being. But ingesting too much alcohol makes the liver become fatty and inflamed, and in some cases, scarred. When that occurs, the damaged liver is no longer able to do its job.

A virtual epidemic of cirrhosis of the liver exists in the United Kingdom, where many pubs and stores that sell liquor are open twenty-four hours a day and sell at very cheap prices. Three-quarters of the young drinkers who have been diagnosed with cirrhosis are women—likely, doctors say, because young women tend to be more sensitive than young men to the harmful effects of alcohol.

In the 1970s cirrhosis claimed approximately twelve hundred lives a year in the United Kingdom. By 2010, however, the toll had climbed to five thousand in a year, and the numbers continue to increase. Warns Professor Ian Gilmore, an expert in liver disease, "We could see up to a quarter of a million preventable deaths from liver disease in the next 20 years."[49]

The High Risk of Brain Damage

But the most worrisome physical problem that can result from chronic use of alcohol—especially at the rate at which many adolescents drink—is brain damage. The brains of teenagers are years away from being completely developed, so damage

When a person develops cirrhosis of the liver, healthy liver tissue (left) is replaced with scar tissue (right). The scar tissue prevents the liver from functioning properly, a condition that can be fatal.

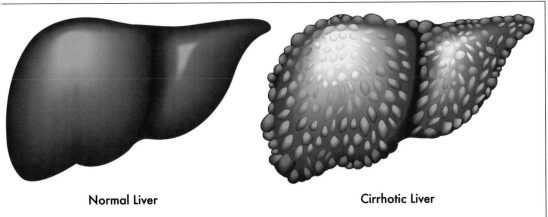

Normal Liver   Cirrhotic Liver

"A Terrible Way to Go"

The death of Stacey Rhymes, a twenty-four-year-old from Nottingham, England, is a cautionary tale for young binge drinkers. She died of cirrhosis of the liver after drinking heavily since the age of seventeen. Her mother, Louise, says that Stacey, lying in her hospital bed, was cuddling a favorite toy from her childhood when she reached out to her mother, asking her to hold her hand. Stacey slipped into a coma, and within a few hours she was dead from abdominal bleeding and liver disease.

Says Louise, "I now want the world to know exactly what happened to Stacey and why. . . . Her stomach was like a balloon, as if she was nine months pregnant. Her long hair was falling out, her urine was colored black and she could not eat. She was scared to look in the mirror because her eyes were canary yellow. The only way to stop the pain at the end was morphine." Louise adds, "My daughter drank herself to death. . . . It was a terrible way to go."

Quoted in Sue Reid, "Dead at 24: The Tragic Story of How a Young Girl's Life Was Wrecked by Cheap Alcohol," *Daily Mail* (London), August 14, 2008. www.dailymail.co.uk.

to the brain's most vulnerable areas can be permanent. According to the American Medical Association, parts of a teen drinker's brain may be as much as 10 percent smaller than those of a nondrinker.

Neuroscientist Susan Tapert led a study at the University of California–San Diego to investigate the specific types of brain damage underage drinkers experience. As Tapert observed in the study, "Adolescents who engage in binge drinking . . . tend to show some brain abnormalities in their brain's white matter. [Those are] the fibers that connect different parts of our brain."[50]

She also noted that binge drinking that continues for two or three years can result in measurable declines in a teen's memory and thinking processes. These declines are not seen in teenagers who have not drunk heavily during the same time period. Some of these declines occurred in teens who had just twelve drinks within a month's time, leading Tapert to doubt that any safe level of teen alcohol alcohol use exists.

A Genetic Problem?

Another study, this one at the University of Illinois–Chicago College of Medicine, found that underage drinking may have highly damaging influences on children's and teens' genes. A particularly alarming finding was that the damage or stunting of the brain's development may be permanent. The head of the study, Professor Subhash Pandey, wanted to find out if binge drinking presents more serious dangers for adolescents than it does for adults. Pandey and his team used rats to see if intermittently exposing them to alcohol in their adolescence would have serious effects as the rats aged.

The team modeled teen binge drinking by giving twenty-eight-day-old rats alcohol for two days in a row, followed by two days with no alcohol. They repeated that pattern for thirteen days. The team followed some of the rats, along with non-drinking rats, into adulthood, observing them carefully for any signs of unusual or abnormal behavior. Both sets of rats were offered a choice of water or alcohol, and the scientists kept careful track of which one they chose.

Teen Choices, Adult Problems

The results of the experiment were unsettling, though not entirely unexpected. The adolescent rats that chose alcohol over water were far more likely to binge drink as they aged. These rats also demonstrated a great deal of anxiety and an increased risk of alcoholism and other negative behaviors—characteristics that are common in humans who have a history of heavy drinking.

Even more interesting, however, were the subsequent findings from the experiment. In an effort to understand if there was a physical explanation for the binge-drinking rats' increased likelihood of becoming alcoholics, Pandey and his team examined brain tissue from those rats to see whether any abnormalities had resulted from their heavy alcohol intake. This research focused on the amygdala, the small, almond-shaped part of the brain that is key to normal growth and maturation in both rats and humans.

Pandey found that the drinking rats' amygdalae were clearly damaged, and the important genetic material that is responsible for communicating inherited traits was unable to do its job. As a result, information that is necessary for the adolescent rats to develop into adult rats was not being processed by their genes—and that failure led to the rats' heightened anxiety and preference for alcohol as adults.

In March 2015 Pandey noted in the journal *Neurobiology of Disease* that his findings—though they were based on the results of using rats—may explain the negative effects that heavy alcohol use can have on a developing human teen brain. "This may be the mechanism," he wrote, "through which adolescent binge-drinking increases the risk for psychiatric disorders, including alcoholism, in adulthood."[51]

Not all effects of alcohol are as dangerous as those discovered by Pandey and his team. However, his research is still more evidence that alcohol's effects can last far beyond vomiting, dizziness, and poor decision making during and directly after the time a person drinks. Many of alcohol's effects may be permanent, leaving lasting damage throughout the rest of a young drinker's life.

Chapter Four

How Can Society Deal with Underage Drinking?

The growing problems associated with teen drinking have forced communities to try to figure out the best way to deal with such issues. Since so many teens have made the choice to drink, it is important to find solutions that can propel them to make a better, wiser choice about alcohol use.

Some of these solutions may involve new laws and regulations designed to discourage teens from choosing to drink, whereas others involve no new laws but rather promote more vigorous enforcement of laws that already exist. Still other ideas have created cutting-edge educational tools for teens and their parents that can more dramatically illustrate the dangers of underage drinking.

Learning to Handle Peer Pressure

Because peer pressure is one of the top reasons teens take their first drink, it makes sense to address the power of peer pressure to try to make it less likely that teens will drink before they are of legal age. Many middle schools and junior high schools are including the topic of peer pressure in the curriculum of a health class or current events class. By using role playing, students learn to refuse the offer of something they know is wrong or that could get them into trouble, such as an invitation to a party at which drinking is likely to take place.

"The thing is, kids don't want to come off looking judgmental when they're declining an offer [to a party], even though they are completely sure no parents are going to be there and

In health classes, many schools now cover the topic of peer pressure and how to resist it. Role playing and other exercises can help teens learn ways to refuse offers to drink alcohol.

there will likely be drugs, and almost certainly booze," says Carrie Schwartz, who has taught junior high students for six years. She adds:

> But it's important to be firm, and not apologize. You can say you don't like to drink, or your parents would ground you if they found out. You can also just stick up for yourself, saying that you'd like to do something together sometime, but you really aren't big into drinking. Or you can say your coach [if you're on a team] would bench you if he found out. In the end, being as close

to the truth without being preachy is the best way, and they'll hear you. They might even respect you more. And it does get easier![52]

Limiting the Liquor Suppliers

One important factor in preventing minors from drinking is to make it more difficult for them to obtain alcohol. US laws are clear about the illegality of anyone under twenty-one purchasing or consuming alcohol. In addition, it is illegal for any adult to purchase alcohol for an underage drinker, which is considered contributing to the delinquency of a minor. But however unambiguous the current laws are, they are not effective in preventing alcohol from getting into the hands of underage drinkers, since approximately 53 percent of young people between age twelve and twenty admit to having engaged in drinking. Some suggest that raising penalties against those who buy liquor for teens would likely make many teens choose not to even ask for the favor, knowing an older sibling or friend might get into trouble.

However, some underage drinkers say that even without an older friend or sibling making the purchase, it is never that difficult to get liquor. "Everybody I know has had really good luck just standing around outside a [liquor] store and asking someone as they're going inside if they'd mind getting you what you want," says Darla, a Chicago nineteen-year-old. "I've heard people call it 'Hey Mistering,' and it's really common. It is a little bit of a risk for the person doing the buying, since it's against the law to buy booze for minors, but most of the time the people you ask are cool with it. I mean, they probably Hey Mistered themselves when they were younger, right?"[53]

> "Everybody I know has had really good luck just standing around outside a [liquor] store and asking someone as they're going inside if they'd mind getting you what you want."[53]
>
> —Darla, a nineteen-year-old from Chicago.

To deter such buys, some police departments use sting operations hoping to catch adults buying liquor for teens. In California in 2015 a number of counties used eighteen-year-old decoys who offered adults ten dollars to buy them beer. The adults who accepted the offer were swiftly arrested and fined $1,000 and ordered to do community service. And although it was somewhat gratifying to catch someone breaking the law, says Jennifer Hill of the Department of Alcoholic Beverage Control, it was not the best outcome. "For law enforcement," says Hill, "a successful operation is when someone will not purchase alcohol for the decoys."[54]

Getting Tough with Sellers

All too often, though, underage drinkers do not need assistance from anyone else to purchase alcohol. Instead they merely take advantage of busy or nonchalant clerks. For example, in 2015 a seventeen-year-old in Walton County, Florida, walked into a gas station to get a can of beer. The clerk looked at his license, which clearly identified him as being seventeen. Distracted or uninterested, the clerk glanced at it, handed it back to him, and rang up the beer.

The boy was actually an undercover operative with the county sheriff's office, which was eager to learn which stations were not complying with laws prohibiting sales of liquor to minors. As soon as the teen walked outside with the beer, two deputies arrested the clerk.

Although 90 percent of vendors selling alcohol in Walton County had been doing a good job refusing to sell alcohol to minors, Sheriff Mike Adkinson later told reporters, "I'm a 'trust but verify' kind of guy. I hope we're going to find that we have good compliance from our vendors here."[55]

Blowing the Whistle on Teen Drinking Parties

Another big concern—both for police and some parents—are teen drinking parties. According to Nick DiPietro, an Anne

Arundel County, Maryland, police officer, there is a frustrating misconception among many parents that teen drinking parties are relatively harmless.

"You're intervening into what is basically a gateway drug," DiPietro explains. "There absolutely are studies that show that alcohol being used underage leads to things such as DWIs [driving while intoxicated], domestic violence. . . . We're not out here looking to pad our [arrest] stats; we're out here trying to intervene in kids' partaking in risky behavior and help the general public."[56]

But catching young drinkers is often difficult because teens are usually careful about keeping their drinking plans from parents and other adults. This is a concern in Anne Arundel County, where alcohol use is higher than the national average. To address the problem, a county health department group known as the Northern Lights Against Substance Abuse Coalition has enacted a tip line that allows people to anonymously alert police about an upcoming party at which underage drinking is likely to occur. The information can help police remove those teens from a potentially dangerous situation, as well as also reduce the risk to the community of traffic accidents caused by drunk teenage drivers.

"We're not out here looking to pad our [arrest] stats; we're out here trying to intervene in kids' partaking in risky behavior."[56]

—Nick DiPietro, an Anne Arundel County, Maryland, police officer.

The idea resonated with those who work to keep teens healthy and to prevent teen drinking. "I think the tip line is another piece of an ongoing strategy," says Sandy Smolnicky, a county health specialist. "I think that there are people who do get wind of parties that are going to happen and they would want to stop them."[57]

Educating Parents About Drinking Parties

In some communities one of the most effective means of cutting down on teen drinking parties is the education of parents. As an educational tool, mock drinking parties are being staged for parents so they can see what actually goes on at one. Though many parents may have heard about drinking parties, most are unaware of the amount of liquor consumed, the binge drinking that occurs, and the drinking games and impaired driving that are commonly associated with these events. The idea is that if parents are aware of the things that may take place at such parties, they will be far less willing to allow their home to be a party site—thus making it an easier choice for their teen to decline to host a party or even attend one.

In April 2015 parents in Santa Monica, California, were invited to take part in a mock drinking party. Hosted by the school district, the city of Santa Monica, the Santa Monica Police Department, and several nonprofit agencies working to prevent and treat alcohol abuse in the community, the event began with the parents' thirty-minute walk-through of a staged drinking party. High school students acted out scripted scenes of binge drinking and drinking games. Parents were able to see just what such parties may encompass—from peer pressure to drink more as well as access to drugs. Afterward, they were part of a debriefing in which police, mental health professionals, and school administrators talked about possible ways to change attitudes toward drinking.

"In my experience, people aren't aware about the amount of exposure and peer pressure youth experience when it comes to drugs and alcohol," says Brenda Simmons, director of the Westside Impact Project, one of the hosts of the mock, or reality, party. The reality party effort, she says, is intended to change that. "The goal of the 'It's Too Easy Reality Party' is to create an opportunity for parents, administrators and community leaders to come together to discuss how we can better protect our youth from the misuse and abuse of drugs and alcohol."[58]

Punishing Parents?

Although most parents are appalled at the idea of their teens attending drinking parties, research has found that a substantial number of others are aware that their teens are hosting such

Underage drinkers sometimes ask older friends or siblings to buy them alcohol. Other times they might use a fake ID to buy alcohol.

gatherings. In August 2014 Bettina Friese, a public health researcher at the Prevention Research Center in Oakland, California, completed a study of teen drinking. Over the course of the study, she met with eleven hundred teens living in North Carolina, and 39 percent of them admitted to having hosted at least one party at which alcohol was consumed. Of those 39 percent, 70 percent stated that their parents knew that underage drinking was taking place.

A Learner's Permit for Drinkers?

John McCardell, president of the University of the South in Sewanee, Tennessee, is a strong proponent of lowering the minimum legal drinking age (MLDA) to eighteen. He has proposed an idea for controlling underage drinkers and the damage they can inflict on the nation's highways and on their own health. In a May 2012 *New York Times* article McCardell suggests a sort of "learner's permit" for drinkers. He reminds readers that the United States is one of only four countries in the world that has an MLDA of twenty-one—the others are Indonesia, Mongolia, and Palau. All other nations either have no minimum age or have a lower MLDA, generally eighteen. Some, like France, allow sixteen-year-olds to purchase and drink wine or beer. McCardell writes:

> We should prepare young adults to make responsible decisions about alcohol in the same way we prepare them to operate a motor vehicle, by first educating and then licensing and permitting them to exercise the full privileges of adulthood so long as they demonstrate their ability to observe the law.

> Licensing would work like drivers education—it would involve a permit, perhaps graduated, allowing the holder the privilege of purchasing, possessing, and consuming alcohol, as each state determined, so long as the holder had passed an alcohol education course and observed the alcohol laws of the issuing state.

Quoted in John M. McCardell Jr., "Let Them Drink at 18, with a Learner's Permit," *New York Times*, May 28, 2012.www.nytimes.com.

As a result of these findings, some communities throughout the United States have decided to hold parents accountable for allowing teens to drink in their homes. These communities have instituted hefty fines. If an adult hosts a party at which alcohol is available to teens, he or she can be fined as much as $1,000 for the first offense, and double that if there is another underage drinking party at the home. Officials hope such measures, in addition to reminding parents to be more aware of what goes on in their homes, will make teens less eager to risk having drinking parties that might result in their parents having to pay a stiff fine.

Mock Crashes

Whereas mock parties can educate parents and others about how teenagers abuse alcohol, another type of mock event can give teens themselves a disturbingly realistic look at the consequences of a drunk driving accident. The mock crash is a staged fatal accident—complete with lots of blood. The aim of mock crashes is to show teens the gruesome aftermath of accidents caused by teens who made the choice to drive after drinking. Mock crashes as a teaching tool are becoming common throughout the United States and Canada, and the response has been quite positive.

Mock crash events are usually held at high schools in the spring, before proms and graduation—two occasions that are notorious for underage drinking. The events include police and fire departments, as well as paramedics, towing companies, and even funeral home employees. The events have been getting raves from many teens who say that the experience has made them think in a whole different way about the choices they make about drinking and driving—as well as the impact those choices have on friends, families, and a myriad of other people in their community.

Fake Blood, Real Tears

Edina, Minnesota, police officer Kenna Rofidal has participated in several mock crashes. "To create the staged crash, we get a couple of wrecked cars from the tow truck company that we use," Rofidal says. "The frames are a mess—twisted metal, and the windows—including the windshields—are usually cracked and broken. And if they're not damaged enough, we break out more of the glass, to make the cars look even worse."[59]

Rofidal says that the crucial participants are high school students themselves. She explains:

We often talk to some kids that are in theater, to get them to participate, because they are likely to feel comfortable playing a role—either as an injured or dead passenger, complete with a lot of gory makeup, lots of blood so they look horribly injured. The girls' prom dresses are torn and bloody, and one passenger is positioned so it looks as though she has gone through the windshield of one of the cars. It's eerie—but we want it as realistic as possible.[60]

A student plays the role of an injured passenger during a mock DUI crash. Students who have taken part in such exercises say the experience makes them think differently about drinking and driving.

Seventeen-year-old Jeannie Kirby witnessed a mock crash at her high school in 2014. Several students she knew took part in the event. Even though she had an idea of what to expect, Kirby was surprised at how she felt. She recalls that the experience seemed almost too real:

> You can hear the sirens coming from far off—it's so eerie, because clearly you know it's too late to save them all. There's so much blood, and glass. For me, I remember really losing it first when the fire department used the jaws of life to get this one boy out of the car. And I lost it again when the funeral home hearse shows up and loads one of the girls in the back. I started crying like crazy—it still gives me goose bumps when I think about it. Even some of the boys who you'd just think would be laughing or screwing around—they're just watching, not talking at all.[61]

Getting Active

In addition to participating in such efforts at the community level, many people become involved in organizations that are working nationwide to eliminate teen alcohol use, and drunk driving especially. One of the most well known of these groups is Mothers Against Drunk Driving, or MADD. The organization was started in 1980 by Candy Lightner, whose thirteen-year-old daughter, Cari, was killed by a drunk driver who swerved into the bike lane where Cari was riding her bicycle. He hit Cari so hard she was hurled 40 yards (37 m) down the road. The driver had been cited three times in the preceding four years for drunk driving, and just two days before killing Cari, he had been arrested for another hit-and-run accident while intoxicated.

> "I started crying like crazy—it still gives me goose bumps when I think about it."[61]
>
> —Jeannie Kirby, a spectator at a mock crash event.

Grieving her daughter's death and outraged that the man was still driving despite his record, Lightner began an organization to advocate harsher legal penalties for drunk drivers. Over the past thirty-five years, MADD's targets have expanded to include drugged driving as well as drunk driving. In 2015 the organization's website announced, "The mission of Mothers Against Drunk Driving is to end drunk driving, help fight drugged driving, support the victims of these violent crimes and prevent underage drinking."[62]

> "After I spoke, a student came up to me and hugged me. . . . She showed nothing but gratitude."[63]
>
> —Juan De La Garza, a MADD volunteer.

One MADD volunteer, Juan De La Garza, became involved with the organization after his seventeen-year-old sister, Alejandra—the mother of a young son—was killed by a drunk nineteen-year-old driver. De La Garza says that after the accident, he made it his mission to educate teens and parents about the dangers of underage drinking and driving and to make sure that no other family has to endure the tragedy that his family has suffered. He says that one particular event at a local high school made him realize that his message was getting through to some students:

After I spoke, a student came up to me and hugged me. There, in a gymnasium full of strangers, a young 17-year-old girl cried on me. She showed nothing but gratitude. When I asked why she cried or why she thanked me, the only thing she could say was "Your sister's story touched me, it opened my eyes. I never want to put my parents in that position. I never want to lose a friend. I want to make the right choice, and stay above the influence." In that very moment I knew out of the 1,000 students present that day, my job was done. One life changed, one [fewer] teen drinking, one young life deciding to be responsible. All because of my sister's life.[63]

Lowering the Drinking Age?

One of the most radical ideas about how to reduce underage drinking is to lower the MLDA in all states from twenty-one to eighteen. The idea seems contradictory to many people. But proponent John McCardell, president of the University of the South in Sewanee, Tennessee, believes that when the MLDA was raised to twenty-one, it merely drove underage drinkers behind closed doors and into the shadows. This led to destructive behaviors such as binge drinking and drunk driving that he has witnessed all too often as a college president.

To gain support for this proposal, McCardell founded a nonprofit organization called Choose Responsibility. The aim of the

Getting MADD

According to the MADD website, many parents who have lost a child or teen to a motor accident involving a drunk driver have found it meaningful to join the organization and work to raise awareness of the dangers of drunk and distracted driving. That was true of the parents of both twenty-three-year-old Eric Fischer and his girlfriend, twenty-year-old Andrea Herrera. On October 10, 2013, while on their way to his house to take care of the puppy they had recently adopted, a drunk driver ran a red light and slammed into their car. The impact pushed the car into the path of a truck, and both Fischer and Herrera were killed.

After the crash, the families connected with MADD's Michigan chapter. The MADD victim advocate, Stephanie Hurst, assisted them in preparing for the trial and even accompanied them to the trial for support. The drunk driver, who had a history of alcohol-related offenses, was found guilty and received a sentence of twelve to thirty years in prison.

The Fischer and Herrera families are adamant that the loss and heartbreak they experienced not happen to another family. They joined the event Walk Like MADD in Grand Rapids, Michigan, to raise money for educational programs to put a stop to drunk driving.

organization is to stimulate informed discussion and debate about the presence of alcohol in American culture and to help young people between eighteen and twenty years old learn to make wise decisions about the use of alcohol.

Many find the idea of lowering the MLDA nationwide outrageous. "The first time I heard that, I was speechless," says James McIntyre, a retired high school teacher. "How exactly would it be safer to have drunk 18-year-olds driving around than drunk 21-year-olds driving around? You're talking about giving permission to drink to kids who are three years younger—and are less mature—than the 21-year-olds that are already a problem now!"[64]

What Is the Answer?

A similar idea, proposed by Minnesota state representative Phyllis Kahn, is to allow bars and restaurants to serve liquor to customers age eighteen and over. Kahn wants to allow young people to learn to drink socially as they do in Europe—without the danger of binge drinking. Wisconsin has a similar law, which allows people as young as eighteen to drink in bars as long as they are with their parents.

Many experts believe it makes a great deal of sense to allow younger people to drink responsibly in the presence of family, just as they do in many European countries. For instance, in France and Italy children as young as seven are often encouraged to have small tastes of wine with family meals on special occasions. The idea is not to get drunk, but to incorporate moderate alcohol use as a normal part of life.

Introducing alcohol early to children in this way makes them far less likely to have problems related to alcohol later, says Brown University anthropology professor Dwight Heath. "[This way] alcohol has no mystique," Heath says. "It's no big deal. By contrast, where it's banned until 21, there's something of the 'forbidden fruit' syndrome."[65]

A Choice with Life-Changing Consequences

Society is adamant about finding solutions to the underage drinking problem because of the life-changing consequences it can have on young people. Though underage drinkers often feel they are invincible, some—like Jessica Rasdall, who chose to drive drunk and caused an accident in which her best friend, Laura Gorman, died—found out that this is not true.

"I miss Laura so much," Rasdall said nearly five years after the accident. "I know she paid the ultimate price and I have the rest of my life ahead of me. But I have to wake up every morning without my best friend, and the devastating knowledge that I killed her. That's my life sentence."[66]

Introduction: A Choice for Teens

1. Carrie, telephone interview with the author, March 8, 2015.

2. Carrie, interview.

3. Carrie, interview.

Chapter One: The Faces of Underage Drinking

4. Quoted in Ronald Reagan Presidential Library & Museum, "Remarks on Signing a National Minimum Drinking Age Bill, July 17, 1984," transcript. www.reagan.utexas.edu.

5. Caron Treatment Centers, "Teenage Underage Drinking," 2015. www.caron.org.

6. Quoted in Heather Millar, "The Hidden Epidemic of Very Young Alcoholics," WebMD, February 1, 2008. www.web md.com.

7. Suzanne, personal interview with the author, February 18, 2015.

8. Suzanne, interview.

9. Ben, telephone interview with the author, February 19, 2015.

10. Quoted in Felicity Thompson, "Teenagers Turning to Alcohol to Relieve Boredom," *Nursing Times*, August 5, 2009. www.nursingtimes.net.

11. Stan, telephone interview with the author, April 1, 2015.

12. Kirsten Dawson, personal interview with the author, March 11, 2015.

13. Piper, personal interview with the author, May 3, 2015.

14. Marvin Smith, personal interview with the author, May 3, 2015.

15. Right Step, "These Dangerous Drinking Games Are Killing Teens," March 26, 2015. www.rightstep.com.

16. Quoted in Peter Wilkinson and Isa Soares, "Neknominate: 'Lethal' Drinking Game Sweeps Social Media," CNN, February 18, 2014. www.cnn.com.

17. Quoted in Carnegie Mellon University, "Press Release: Teens Who Drink Alone More Likely to Develop Alcohol Problems as Young Adults, Carnegie Mellon and University of Pittsburgh Researchers Find," November 18, 2013. www.cmu.edu.

18. Lloyd Mueller, telephone interview with the author, May 28, 2015.

19. Quoted in Millar, "The Hidden Epidemic of Very Young Alcoholics."

20. Quoted in British Liver Trust, "Liver Disease Timebomb for Young Drinkers," November 25, 2013. www.britishliver trust.org.uk.

21. Marvin Smith, personal interview with the author, May 28, 2015.

Chapter Two: Factors That Influence Underage Drinking

22. National Institute on Alcohol Abuse and Alcoholism, "Underage Drinking: A Major Public Health Challenge," *Alcohol Alert*, April 2003. http://pubs.niaaa.nih.gov.

23. Allie, personal interview with the author, March 22, 2015.

24. Allie, interview.

25. Allie, interview.

26. Elizabeth Berg, telephone interview with the author, March 19, 2015.

27. Paul Sjorensen, telephone interview with the author, March 19, 2015.

28. Quoted in "Parental Messages That Stress No Alcohol Do Get Through, Survey Finds," HealthDay, April 1, 2014. http://consumer.healthday.com.

29. Justin, personal interview with the author, March 18, 2015.

30. Greg, telephone interview with the author, April 3, 2015.

31. William Lowe, telephone interview with the author, May 1, 2015.

32. University of Pittsburgh Medical Center, "Pitt Study Finds U.S. Kids Heavily Exposed to Alcohol Brands in Music," October 18, 2011. www.upmc.com.

33. Quoted in Nuzha Nuseibeh, "Teen Binge Drinking Linked to Pop Music Alcohol References, but Is This Really Surprising?," *Bustle*, April 12, 2014. www.bustle.com.

34. Quoted in Tom Roland, "Does Country Music Need an Alcohol Intervention?," *Billboard*, July 29, 2014. www.billboard.com.

35. Tracy, personal interview with the author, April 16, 2015.

36. Quoted in Lucy Wallis, "Is 25 the New Cut-Off Point for Adulthood?," BBC, September 23, 2013. www.bbc.com.

37. Quoted in Richard Knox, "The Teen Brain: It's Just Not Grown Up Yet," NPR, March 1, 2010. www.npr.org.

38. Quoted in Doug Carlson, "Teenage Brain: Studies Explain Risky Behavior," Florida State University, August 28, 2014. www.fsu.edu.

Chapter Three: What Are the Consequences of Underage Drinking?

39. Ellie Adams, telephone interview with the author, March 17, 2015.

40. Quoted in Buddy T, "Teen's Death Exposes Binge Drinking Dangers," About Health, November 28, 2014. http://alcoholism.about.com.

41. Quoted in *DrexelNow* (Drexel University), "Q&A with Taylor Anderson: The Dangers of Binge Drinking for Women," January 16. 2013. www.drexel.edu.

42. Quoted in Aviva Shen, "Accused Rapists Scribbled Messages All Over 15-Year-Old Audrie Pott's Unconscious Body," *ThinkProgress* (blog), April 16, 2013. http://think progress.org.

43. Quoted in Shen, "Accused Rapists Scribbled Messages All Over 15-Year-Old Audrie Pott's Unconscious Body."

44. Quoted in Tara Fowler, "Teens Settle with Family of 15-Year-Old Who Committed Suicide Following Sexual Assault," *People*, April 7, 2015. www.people.com.

45. Steven, personal interview with the author, May 1, 2015.

46. Darren, personal interview with the author, May 1, 2015.

47. Quoted in Drinkaware, "Alcohol and Aggression," March 2015. www.drinkaware.co.uk.

48. Adams, interview.

49. Quoted in British Liver Trust, "Liver Disease Timebomb for Young Drinkers."

50. Quoted in Michelle Trudeau, "With Drinking, Parent Rules Do Affect Teens' Choices," NPR, May 31, 2010. www.npr .org.

51. Quoted in Sharon Parmet, "Adolescent Drinking Affects Adult Behavior Through Genetic Changes," UIC News Center, April 2, 2015. http://news.uic.edu.

Chapter Four: How Can Society Deal with Underage Drinking?

52. Carrie Schwartz, personal interview with the author, May 28, 2015.

53. Darla, telephone interview with the author, April 30, 2015.

54. Quoted in Zohreen Adamjee, "Statewide Sting Busts Adults Buying Alcohol for Minors," Fox 5, March 14, 2015. http://fox5sandiego.com.

55. Quoted in Trista Pruett, "Underage Drinking: Deputies Try to Nip Sales in the Bud," *Northwest Florida Daily News* (Fort Walton Beach, FL), April 3, 2015. www.nwfdailynews.com.

56. Quoted in Brandi Bottalico, "County Sets Up Tip Line for Teen Drinking Parties," *Annapolis (MD) Capital Gazette*, March 5, 2015. www.capitalgazette.com.

57. Quoted in Bottalico, "County Sets Up Tip Line for Teens Drinking Parties."

58. Quoted in Hector Gonzalez, "Mock Party in Santa Monica Targets Underage Drinking," *Santa Monica Lookout*, April 22, 2015. www.surfsantamonica.com.

59. Kenna Rofidal, personal interview with the author, May 5, 2015.

60. Rofidal, interview.

61. Jeannie Kirby, personal interview with the author, May 4, 2015.

62. MADD, "Mission Statement," 2015. www.madd.org.

63. Juan De La Garza, "#TributeTuesday: Alejandra De La Garza," MADD35, April 14, 2015. www.madd.org.

64. James McIntyre, telephone interview with the author, April 30, 2015.

65. Quoted in Brandon Griggs, "Should the U.S. Lower Its Drinking Age?," CNN, January 4, 2015. www.cnn.com.

66. Jessica Rasdall, "Experience: I Killed My Best Friend," *Guardian* (Manchester), December 16, 2011. www.theguardian.com.

Al-Anon/Alateen

1600 Corporate Landing Pkwy.
Virginia Beach, VA 23454-5617
phone: (613) 723-8484
e-mail: wso@al-anon.org

These organizations offer fellowship to people who are suffering from alcoholism or who have family members that are suffering from alcoholism. Al-Anon is geared for adults, whereas Alateen is for teenagers.

American Council on Alcoholism

1000 E. Indian School Rd.
Phoenix, AZ 85014
phone: (800) 527-5344
e-mail: info@aca-usa.org
website: www.aca-usa.org

This organization is a referral service for people who suffer from alcoholism, as well as for their families, treatment professionals, and others who are interested in learning more about alcohol dependence, alcohol abuse, and options for recovery.

DrinkingAndDriving.org

18275 Grove Pl.
Fontana, CA 92336
phone: (888) 502-3236
website: www.drinkinganddriving.org

DrinkingAndDriving.org is dedicated to preventing drunk driving, especially among teenagers. The organization provides education and important tools such as information about services that will drive home people who have been drinking.

Mothers Against Drunk Driving (MADD)

511 E. John Carpenter Fwy., No. 700
Irving, TX 75062
phone: (800) 438-6223
e-mail: info@madd.org
website: www.madd.org

MADD is dedicated to putting an end to drunk driving, preventing underage drinking, and supporting victims of drunk driving accidents.

National Institute on Alcohol Abuse and Alcoholism (NIAAA)

National Institutes of Health
5635 Fishers Ln., MSC 9304
Bethesda, MD 20892-9304

The NIAAA, part of the National Institutes of Health, supports and conducts research on alcohol's impact on human health and well-being. It is the world's largest funder of alcohol research.

Students Against Destructive Decisions (SADD)

SADD National
255 Main St.
Marlborough, MA 01752
phone: (877) 723-3462
website: www.sadd.org

Though SADD has long been an organization that works to prevent underage drinking, it now addresses the dangers of drinking and driving among teens. SADD has thousands of local chapters throughout the United States.

For Further Research

Books

Marylou Ambrose and Veronica Deisler, *Investigate Alcohol.* Berkeley Heights, NJ: Enslow, 2015.

Donna Cornett, *Beat Binge Drinking: A Smart Drinking Guide for Teens, College Students and Young Adults Who Choose to Drink.* Santa Rosa, CA: People Friendly, 2011.

Amitava Dasgupta, *The Science of Drinking: How Alcohol Affects Your Body and Mind.* Lanham, MD: Rowman & Littlefield, 2011.

Barron Lerner, *One for the Road: Drunk Driving Since 1900.* Baltimore: Johns Hopkins University Press, 2011.

Mark E. Rose and Cheryl J. Cherpitel, *Alcohol: Its History, Pharmacology, and Treatment.* Center City, MN: Hazelden Foundation, 2011.

Periodicals and Internet Sources

Malcolm Gladwell, "Drinking Games," *New Yorker*, February 15, 2010.

Ann Lewis Hamilton, "Rethinking the Drinking Age," *Huffington Post*, March 26, 2015. www.huffingtonpost.com/ann-lewis-hamilton/rethinking-the-drinking-age_b_6941674.html.

Emily Listfield, "The Underage Drinking Epidemic," *Parade,* June 13, 2011.

Websites

Alcohol Awareness Research Library (www.alcoholstats .com). This website has helpful statistics and information about underage drinking and drunk driving.

Cool Spot (www.thecoolspot.gov). This is a helpful, age-appropriate site for teens, with facts about alcohol and the risks of alcohol abuse, along with tips on how to resist peer pressure.

Stop Underage Drinking (www.stopalcoholabuse.com). This detailed website provides information on underage drinking and a range of programs operated by the federal government to combat underage drinking.

Index

Note: Boldface page numbers indicate illustrations.

Picture Credits

Cover: Thinkstock Images

Depositphotos: 26, 39, 47

Roger Harries/Science Photo Library: 34

iStock: 15

© Marcio Jose Sanchez/AP/Corbis: 42

Shutterstock: 30, 57

© Steve Marcus/Reuters/Corbis: 19

Thinkstock Images: 8, 11, 52, 60

Gail Stewart is the author of more than 180 books for children, teens, and young adults. She and her husband live in Minneapolis, Minnesota, and are the parents of three grown sons.